Sandpaper & Seahorses

John Froy was born in Yorkshire and grew up in the West Country. He went to art school, travelled widely, and taught English as a Foreign Language. He settled in Reading with his wife and daughter and started a decorating business. He ran Two Rivers Press for a number of years. He has published *Eggshell: A Decorator's Notes* and a memoir *The Art School Dance* with Two Rivers, and two further volumes of memoir. *Sandpaper & Seahorses* is his second poetry collection.

Other books by the same author

Eggshell: A Decorator's Notes, Two Rivers Press (2007)
Waterloo Road: A Childhood Memoir 1953–1970, Pine Wave Press (2010)
The Art School Dance, Two Rivers Press (2013)
Teacher, Squatter, City Farmer, self-published (2018)

Also by Two Rivers poets

David Attwooll, *The Sound Ladder* (2015)
Kate Behrens, *The Beholder* (2012)
Kate Behrens, *Man with Bombe Alaska* (2016)
Adrian Blamires, *The Pang Valley* (2010)
Adrian Blamires & Peter Robinson (eds.), *The Arts of Peace* (2014)
David Cooke, *A Murmuration* (2015)
Terry Cree, *Fruit* (2014)
Claire Dyer, *Eleven Rooms* (2013)
Claire Dyer, *Interference Effects* (2016)
A. F. Harrold, *The Point of Inconvenience* (2013)
Ian House, *Nothing's Lost* (2014)
Gill Learner, *The Agister's Experiment* (2011)
Gill Learner, *Chill Factor* (2016)
Sue Leigh, *Chosen Hill* (2018)
Becci Louise, *Octopus Medicine* (2017)
Mairi MacInnes, *Amazing Memories of Childhood, etc.* (2016)
Steven Matthews, *On Magnetism* (2017)
Henri Michaux, *Storms under the Skin* translated by Jane Draycott (2017)
Tom Phillips, *Recreation Ground* (2012)
John Pilling & Peter Robinson (eds.), *The Rilke of Ruth Speirs:
    New Poems, Duino Elegies, Sonnets to Orpheus & Others* (2015)
Peter Robinson, *English Nettles and Other Poems* (2010)
Peter Robinson (ed.), *Reading Poetry: An Anthology* (2011)
Peter Robinson (ed.), *A Mutual Friend: Poems for Charles Dickens* (2012)
Peter Robinson, *Foreigners, Drunks and Babies: Eleven Stories* (2013)
Lesley Saunders, *Cloud Camera* (2012)
Lesley Saunders, *Nominy-Dominy* (2018)
Robert Seatter, *The Book of Snow* (2016)
Susan Utting, *Fair's Fair* (2012)
Susan Utting, *Half the Human Race* (2017)
Jean Watkins, *Scrimshaw* (2013)

Sandpaper & Seahorses

John Froy

First published in the UK in 2018 by Two Rivers Press
7 Denmark Road, Reading RG1 5PA
www.tworiverspress.com

© John Froy 2018

The right of the poet to be identified as the author of this work
has been asserted by him in accordance with the Copyright,
Designs and Patents Act of 1988.

All rights reserved. No part of this publication may be reproduced,
stored in or introduced into a retrieval system, or transmitted,
in any form, or by any means (electronic, mechanical, photocopying,
recording or otherwise) without the prior written permission
of the publisher.

ISBN 978-1-909747-38-8

1 2 3 4 5 6 7 8 9

Two Rivers Press is represented in the UK by Inpress Ltd
and distributed by NBNi.

Cover painting: Detail from Long Wiltshire Landscape by Martin Froy, 1976
Text and cover design by Nadja Guggi and typeset in Janson and Parisine

Printed and bound in Great Britain by Imprint Digital, Exeter

Acknowledgements

I would like to thank members of Stones Room, Top Storey and Thin Raft
writing groups for their continuing inspiration, and Adrian Blamires for
his help with the manuscript.

My thanks also to the editors of the following publications where some
of these poems have appeared: *Homesickness and Exile* (Emma Press),
Tales from our Town (Reading Writers), *Reading Poetry* (Two Rivers Press),
Reading University Creative Arts, *South*, *Boomslang*, *The Unruly Sun*,
Pendulum, *RAF 100 Group* magazine. The poem 'Home' won 3rd prize
in the South Downs Poetry Competition 2016.

For my departed father and stepfather

Contents

Every Grain of Rice and the Old Cook | 1
Learning of my Father's Illness | 2
Miroirs | 2
Eden Project | 3
One Spring Morning | 4
Photos I Couldn't Take in Costa Rica | 5
The New Mudlarks | 6
Today my heart went out | 6
Born | 7
Someone I've Never Seen in My Life | 8
Pear Drops | 8
Hokusai's Wave | 9
Another Dream | 9
Poem on Sandpaper | 10
Season Ticket | 10
The Lingering | 11
Message from Down Under | 11
Uxorious | 12
Treasure | 12
By a Leaking Pond | 13
Bad Science | 13
Home | 14
Shackleton's Whisky | 15
The tits go mad in the trees | 16
When All Risk of Frost has Passed | 16
Gardening with Tights | 17
Days with Bulifanyoo | 18
Dinton Pastures | 20
Wolf | 21
The Cigar | 22
The Baroness's Daughter | 23
The House in Cumbria | 24
Still Laid Up in Cumbria | 25
Lay-by | 26
And it was worth it after all | 26
The Share | 27

Subject of Painting | 28
A Boat called Groucho | 29
Old Pennies | 30
In the Hospice Shop | 31
December Postcard | 31
Her Last Hour | 32
Common Prayer | 33
Alison's Lilies | 34
In Summer Don't Hoover | 34
The Artist's Last Birthday | 35
We Thought the World of Him | 35
Quietest Road in England | 36
The Outfit | 37
Reaching Out | 38
Love that Man | 39
The Sexiness of Airports | 40
And I Like the Way | 41
First Visit to Japan | 42
Haiku string | 43
26.4.11 (Waiting for Fukushima) | 44
Charm of Goldfinches | 45
A Kite for Oscar | 45
The Naming of Wagtails | 46
Wing-mirror Spider | 47
Opportunists | 48
In-flight Refreshment | 49
Seahorse | 50
The Love | 51
Pacuare Reserve | 52
To the Ocean | 53
Sargasso | 54

Every Grain of Rice and the Old Cook
on the eve of the Climate Change Conference

These days I'll retrieve a single grain
to add to the risotto pan

as a Japanese grandmother advised,
remembering post-war days.

If we chewed each mouthful thirty-two times,
she growled, we'd all live longer lives.

My deft fingers find this no trouble at all.
There are seventeen drops in the empty bottle.

Learning of my Father's Illness

He's struck by my sun hat, hurries
through the old house to put his on.
On the terrace, he hands me a tiny note:
doctors' names, daffodils, a capital A.

My head swims in the rocking seat.
It showed on the scan last year –
he didn't say: *What a lot of fuss*.
Now he's as open as he's ever been

taking me to the garden shed, warm
with creosote, smoke and oil
before the taxi came. His famous last
words are more precious than ever:

*Border shears a bit blunt, if you
miss a bit, then just go back. I find
it makes such a difference to have
the lawn all trimmed and right.*

Miroirs

Dad, you've taken up late-night piano
playing without a score. I can hear
the chink of the many glasses you polished,
laid out with such decorum and care –
your surprising dream to be a wine waiter.

Eden Project

So I trip off down the zigzag path,
back in time, into the old clay pit
that is reborn. It's early but light,
the lime-green of springtime,
glassy pear tree leaves against blue sky.
If there could be a place that explores
what a great future might look like.
An unknown bird staccatos.
I read the signs along the way.
More trees – more wood – more carbon
locked up – less CO^2 in the air – cooler world.
A yellow digger roars below,
tearing up the ground.
We apologise for disruption caused
by essential building before the season.
An inferno down on the torn earth,
fresh diesel stink, particulates.
Filled with the fear of here and now
I can no longer hear or smell or think.

One Spring Morning

Shadows shrink across the room
as I look out at the hard bright sun,

you reading in bed in your Chinese gown,
and I tell you about it, how the town

was quiet after the panic and confusion
of taking our girl down to the station –

news of closures, a police cordon …
suicide, bomb or misinformation –

and my usual sadness became tinged with joy,
found new strength in seeing her walk away

through the swing doors of that cavernous place
without a single backward glance –

the sun has moved round to pour on your face,
a blackcap is singing, flown in from France.

Photos I Couldn't Take in Costa Rica

Nosing through the water hyacinth,
a bright green iguana, gimlet-eyed,
motionless, matched to the green of the stems,
sets us rocking in the creek.

Or bumping along plantation road,
the young Brahmin cow, suede brown,
up to the haunches in a grassy swamp,
on her hump a skinny white egret.

Now shabby tin hut on stilts
adorned with lines of small bright clothes,
family of ten looking out from the stoop.
We didn't stop.

Nor in the rushing light and shade of an iron bridge
where dozens bathe in their clothes –
the poor, reminder it's Sunday on the river.
What chance of catching that?

Any more than that other bridge of touts,
car parks, merchandise, police,
where tourists gasp over railings
at truly enormous American crocodiles.

And poorest barrio of all, edge of the capital,
hemmed-in shacks, chaos of wiring, dust.
Why? Why take that?
To show to the rich?

The New Mudlarks

Once again on these muddy shores
where kites were common, oysters humble,
one man's junk is another's joy.
The chase is on for us today
in our brave new world of waste.

We few work with plants, the cast out,
potbound, leggy. Come to rescue
what was grown and didn't sell.
Gather them up, take them home,
this is my kind of hunting.

They know us at the garden centre
for the big seasonal markdowns
(all clematis one pound).
To spread them, diversify species
we snap them up like hungry carp.

Like the night fox scenting city trash,
returned red kites' razor vision,
we forage through skip and Grundon
in urgent mission to recycle.

Today my heart went out

to a 150-year-old halibut
landed in Norway, strung up
with its odd, lopsided smile.

Born

On the shore of a northern lake
Reclining Woman by Henry Moore,
huge-thighed, holed, verdigrised.

Teazles scratched my arms and legs,
cool air rushing past,
I pitched forward on my face.

Sycamore seeds helicoptered round
the boy on the windy common
where so many things were forbidden –

anthill seat of swarming reds,
itching powder, goosegrass and worse,
the postbox too far down the lane.

And inching out over the canal,
waterfall of his dream, Niagara,
pulled him to its dread glass lip.

A gas main blew in the night,
blasted a house they knew to bits,
lit up his room like a nuclear test.

This sweet stalk to chew, dung to poke,
I'm raised from the bright sward,
carried up the hill in her arms.

The search goes ever on,
working back to where we come from.

Someone I've Never Seen in My Life

greeted me from across the street.
'Do I know you?' I asked.
'I know you,' he laughed, indicating
with his thumb back along the way.

In the waiting room I spent some time
trying to recall ... Mark, Simon, Paul?
He seemed so certain of me,
yet nothing was familiar about him.

I came out of there backwards,
turned and followed the road he'd shown,
looking in front gardens, uncurtained windows,
in all the open doors I could find.

Pear Drops

Once I sucked pear drops to a spear, pineapple chunks to a blade,
stole the sharp scissors and snipped off his dahlias in a rage;
lost a parent, gained one, changed towns, shrank and grew,
learnt to cycle with no hands down the hill from school;
pinched things from Woolworths I didn't really need,
could feel inside her blouse but not in her jeans;
sat crosslegged with my corkscrew hair tuned in to Quintessence,
dared cross a sign over the highway – crawled back in penance;
wore evening dress to the art school dance and met an Irish American,
swam in the midnight harbour for my jackdaw-haired woman;
had a bad trip: something like hell hovering by my shoulder,
then I stopped a second *copa* and saw you walk away for ever.

Hokusai's Wave

My love, it's only 2:23
in this night of eternity,
the insanity of my life at sea.
Please, please, I cannot sleep.

All the usual ploys: sheep
through hoops, thee thee thee,
alternate nostril breathing,
reading poetry.

In March off Sendai
claw of wave enfolding,
writhing, seething, grinding –
the towering tsunami.

Through the pre-dawn chill
a scene replayed, endlessly.

Another Dream

Heart flutters at my desk
like a passerine in a mist net
held in the fist of the ringer.

I'm only halfway across the playing field
spread-eagled on the bright green grass
The Walrus playing through my head.

Poem on Sandpaper

That picture of a fifteen-year-old boy
on a tree in the New Forest yesterday,
toes almost touching the ground.
The story of a mother who lay under a train
at Braintree, on the same stretch of track
as her daughter had a month before –
these things I scribble with a carpenter's stub
on a piece of coarse grit, the only paper
to hand. So glad you'll be home tonight.

Season Ticket

On the shiny station concourse
among pin suits and announcements,
I chomp a rosy windfall, scrumped
from a wild orchard not a mile from here.
There's nowhere to put the core
in all this glass and steel, so I eat it too.

Bladder. Pancreas. Lung. Throat.
Friends gone or on their way.
The longer you stick around
the more it strikes, naturally.
Five-year, annual, monthly, weekly,
which will see me through?

The Lingering

Hands still large, soft painter's fingers
but he's smaller in the new room,
arms and legs now broccoli stalks,
purple-veined.

His body twisted into the bed
from another TIA,
clouded eyes in lashless sockets
crying to my soul.

'Help! Help me!' he shouts in my ear,
jumping me from the chair.
Painkillers worn thin.
'Fucking awful, it's been!'
Swearing I've never heard from him.

There's nothing to be done but
go find a nurse, tell them he's worse.

Message from Down Under

Life is sad and rum
now my old friend Graeme
can no longer have a jar with me
Tuesday afternoons.

Dispiriting, he agrees,
but too whisky.
Though he hasn't carked it yet.
Mustn't put the quart
before the hearse, he whispers.
If it can't be fixed with No. 8 wire …
Too late too late, he intones
to his old friend John the Pom.

Uxorious

I'm listening for you in June's ululation:
a pair of dun-coloured collared doves
side by side on the wires, all smoochy,
almost purring in the drowsy afternoon;
while town-loving swifts softly screech,
never collide arrowing through our patch of sky
so blue today against the brick.
How the buzz of bees is magnified
inside each pollen-drenched flower.
A family of long-tails churr and fuss
in the branches above my bench.
I'll mow the lawn close for you, add armfuls
of grass clippings to the compost ferment.
We needn't go anywhere for all of this.

Treasure

a capsule of time at end of summer
wedged between hours of motorway driving:
New Hall gardens on Sunday, our bench
among the flaring cannas and dahlias,
glimpse of a black squirrel she said was a grey,
part of the melanomic population there,
and loving her for informing us
while we shared bread and hummus,
split a pomegranate with our fingers.

By a Leaking Pond

She shields her eyes from the morning light,
lashes of clear young eyes soaked through.

The pond's half empty now – *a whole ecosystem will die*,
she cries, carrying the world on her shoulder.

When he told her it was over she fled into the night,
called us from the train to leave the bolt undone.

Eyes glisten again in the warm spring sun,
skaters and water boatmen beginning to move.

Bad Science

My daughter will slaughter me
for the quasi-science, my poesie
dressing up meteorology.
It's bad science to confuse the conditions today
with systems that are centuries old.
When I say we've really buggered the climate now,
it will always be too cold, too hot, too wet, too hurricane,
she snaps, *That's weather, not fucking climate change.*
But primroses out before Christmas, snowdrops
for months, the daffodils not budging this year?

Home

She's flown south to Chile and I keep the image
of her heavy pack, light step on the concourse
looking left and right, but never back.
I drive home, freed too, in a way …

set off walking, am swamped by kids
pouring from school into the winter afternoon,
and looking up see the moon she sees
rising over rooftops in a scintillating sky.

At Sunday lunch I'm suddenly queasy,
carried away to Rothera on the Peninsula
to help the loading of the *James Clark Ross*.
She said it would be a bit military.

The moon's now full and she's been sailing
five days through the Roaring Forties
to reach the home of the great wanderer.
I'll have *The Ancient Mariner* to hand

while she studies senescence in albatrosses,
a season on South Georgia among biting fur seals
weighing, tagging, naming the birds,
climbing daily to the nests in the tussocks.

There's no email and don't expect one, remember
when you were hitching rides on the back of trucks
through the Atacama, with never a message home.

She's on an icebreaker in the Southern Ocean,
but don't think that tree can't fall on you
the next time you open your front door.

Like an Arctic tern, lover of eternal daylight,
she's flying north tomorrow, and the day after,
last leg of the loop, Antarctica and back,
landing at Brize where I'll be with our old car.

Shackleton's Whisky

During the restoration of his base
on Ross Island, a stash was found
buried beneath. Too precious to ship,
a case of this rarest Mackinlay
was flown carefully to New Zealand
to thaw; samples went on to Scotland
for tasting and other testing.

At school, Scott was the red house and won;
yellow Amundsen got there first but may have cheated.
Shackleton was blue and somehow fairest;
we learnt no one had died on his expedition.
This discovery also leads to my mother
and her endurance: a late bottle – of Teachers!
Full! – missed in the posthumous searches,
uncovered at the back of her wardrobe.

Fourteen years on, under the stairs
I admire its deep amber, imagine a rare nose.
'If you don't, someone else will,' she'd say.
And in my temptation I tell her ghost
it doesn't follow, not to be such a slave
to booze, and isn't it funny her granddaughter
is going there now for her PhD.
While in the news Prime Minister John Key
has returned only three of the bottles
to refreeze in that Antarctic hut.

The tits go mad in the trees

In the road this afternoon, it's warmer, lighter – already February,
and as ever I think of you, your birthday. Trees and bushes are alive
with cheesy chatterings: blue tits, great tits, coal tits, all getting it on.

When All Risk of Frost has Passed

Ignoring his advice I plant out
the half-hardys in May.
I'll take a chance with this fickle sun,
overcome weather's vagaries.

The old man remains circumspect,
he will wait until June.
I glimpse him walking his garden,
more measured, taking on less.

For weeks it stays cold and wet.
I'm out there every night
running round with cloche and fleece,
blind in the poker-face of nature.

Over the wall his caution rings
in my ear: *Reckless like your mother,
look what happened there.*

I plant out more. They don't grow,
the nights chill, soil unwarmed;
each morning more tips bitten off.
It seems the frosts will never pass.

Gardening with Tights

So I stretched the legs of a pair of tights,
pushed in fistfuls of barley straw,
tied the top and threw the lot in the pond
for its bacteria to clear the water.

In a Yorkshire greenhouse, a sweet pea fancier
suspends his wife's old tights in rows by colour,
packs each with seed pods which crack when dry
and squeezes them down to the cut-off toe.

On allotments everywhere ponytailed gardeners
are wearing scrunchies made from tights.
They fill tights with earth to build retaining walls,
bag their melons, hang onions to dry.

Soft and strong, you can tie in tomatoes,
climbing roses, line terracotta pots with them.
Or make sieves for jam, mirror wipes,
scrub for bath and sink, a paint strainer
hoover filter, storage for CDs. Cut them
at the thigh and wash delicates inside
or hang sweaters, an arm in each leg
tied to the clothesline. Stretch the waist
round the bin to stop bags slipping down.
At a pinch repair the fan belt.

Fill them with your hair (or your dog's)
and hang on the fence to deter deer.

Days with Bulifanyoo

Oh cantarra, says my father,
why do we have to be here?
The doctor's here.
He's dressed but hasn't got up.

Just get up and go. What is that?
A semblance of me, you,
I wasn't here
like that particular lorry.

I've come fresh from the Red Cross
a new wheelchair in the car,
not knowing if he would know me today.

How are you, Dad?
Oh mustn't. This and. Here and.
Can … tarra … Buli … fany … probably.
Don't understand it at all.
Do you?

I sit with tears and News 24.
'How are you, Dad?'
Oh flutter of a flutter.

Through the lace curtain
gold leaves fall from the sycamore,
Can you see them, Dad? Can you?

Blue skies out in the car park,
you stuck with your stick limbs and nappy in here.

They weren't here, any of us.
Do you get out much?
'I come and see you. When I can.'

It's bright and warm in the room,
the open door, passing nurses.
Daytime is always on.
Yesterday channel up his street.

Extraordinary, buli ..., he gives a kind of salute.
Someone important is here.
It's me! I am the Colonel today.

'Thirsty, Dad?'
What? This? How do I?

Lips grope for the drinking spout.
Not too much at once.
They can forget to swallow
along with everything else.

Oh, here we go. Pout. Glower. Enraged.
Out, out, get out, get away!
'No, Dad, no! Please help!'

Asta, warm-bosomed, 'Always
he get out of the bed. Kill himself.
Tomorrow we go out in wheelchair, Martin.'

He's quiet. 'More water?'
Yes, would you like some?
Forgotten again. At least he can.

We drift further into the afternoon.
He handles the beaker better today,
taps his foot to Bach.

Here come the fervent blown kisses
as I leave, step further into his shoes.

Dinton Pastures

More planes than people, he remarked
as we walked on a blazing June morning,
the path wild through dog roses.
I was taking him to the hide,
that slot view of the lake he liked
where he could sit and rest and chatter.
There were deep red damselflies,
white egrets feeding, and I thought
how it comes round, how he took me
out for a spin before I could drive.
He paused on his stick, the old painter
gazing in wonder at a blue latticed sky,
at the way vapour trails define the space.
A wren churred loudly from the thicket
that last time we went by there.

Wolf

First there was Peter, tiptoeing through the woods,
then a warning at story time to cry only if you meant it.
We both knew that Little Goat who ran away
would be gobbled up when he reached the purple hills.

Tears were only attention-seeking.
I had been fibbing to him all along.
No one would come when you really needed.
They stop listening, you know.

Wide-eyed, the boy set off for that wolf-infested
distance, knowing cries fell on deaf ears.
In the forest of yellow eyes and fangs, he found friends.
When his father died he howled at the moon.

Then he was being wheeled on a gurney.
His heart was wired, his bare head
slid into a steel drum at hospital midnight,
a rubber snake wriggled down to his gut.

False alarms, all – though they had listened.
He went home armed with painkillers,
still wondered when to make the call.

The Cigar

All praised his charity work,
a walk to Land's End from John o' Groats.
He fixed your dreams, raised millions,
seemed a good man in our house.
How about that then.

He's inside my *Top of the Pops*,
the funny one with long white hair,
cigar, close-up lizard skin, tracksuit,
yodelling.
Now then, guys and gals.

Dead mother's room kept as it was,
her clothes dry-cleaned each year,
while the visits to institutions,
children's homes went on and on.
Now then, now then, now then.

Gold coffin encased in concrete (he knew)
tilted forty-five degrees for a view of the sea.
The songs, the songs, he crawled into,
get out your old records and see.
Goodness gracious. As it happens.

The Baroness's Daughter

Eva von Sacha-Masoch, Austrian aristocrat,
lived in Milman Road without a car or phone,
sent her daughter to St Joseph's convent,
charitably subsidised, just along the street

desperate to salvage something
after Major Faithfull, ex-MI6, mad inventor,
threw them out of Brazier's commune,
home to neo-paganism and Woodcraft Folk.

The latchkey child of Holy Jo's.
trudged past here for years, I imagine,
hair up, convent uniform outrageous,
learning from the Index of Banned Books

smuggled in past the nuns, she said.
She joined the young Progress Theatre.
Then ran away to London, and suddenly
'As Tears Go By' was Number One.

She was Jagger's girlfriend, decadence
personified, and scourged by the Press.
I was still at school, but tuning in hard
to all tomorrow's parties.

When I put on my patchouli-oil coat,
she had moved to a Soho wall,
sharing fires on a bombsite in St Anne's Court,
twenty-five heroin jacks on the NHS

from Bell & Croyden, the chemist.
I felt her when I walked those West End streets,
heard her climb back through the songs,
that cracked gravel sound of Kurt Weill.

We played *Broken English* in the language school,
listened in awe to 'Why'd Ya Do It?'
So glad, Marianne, you pulled through,
I still live between the convent and Milman Road.

The House in Cumbria

Dawn, and everything's on the move –
the fine old chest of drawers
slides towards the partition
of ancient timber panelling.
A chair sidles over worm-riddled boards
that slope towards these thick rubble walls.
My bed-frame crackles like musket fire
each time I move; edges south and east
and through the deep-set window
to a spectral wood, cobwebbed.

Captain Edward Ashford Wild,
great granddad, I'm under your spell –
stowed away inside your sea-chest
with camphor smells and rosewood,
a leather writing-top, pigeon-holes.
Aboard the *Pioneer*, bound for Bombay
and the Moluccas, sun still not risen.

Still Laid Up in Cumbria

Sleepy head, the sun is up
but I'm to spend another day in bed
with pictures propped against the wall,
a passed-down wardrobe stuffed full.

Shouts in the field, the long phone call.
I like that your books are still unsorted,
stacked in random, dangerous piles.
New windows without blinds widen the view.

Last night the horses were restless
in the yard. I waited for headlights,
clang of the gate, didn't know if you came.
Now you're out moving the electric fence.

More rest, doctor's orders.
I mind-film crimson cyclamen on the sill,
late summer oaks across the stream,
follow the crazy crack in the ceiling.

There's plenty of making good to do.
I'll repair the torn woodchip for you,
fix that patch of rising damp. Muck out.
Brave ticks and horseflies in the paddock.

Lay-by

You might know it on the A303,
a respite after Stonehenge.
Eyes peeled over one more hill
till the last brow, speed camera, Little Chef,
and there: smelly portaloo, bacon roll,
tea in styrofoam, crusted sugar spoon.
We park among the haulage and bikers,
individual motors: MG, Hillman, Triumph,
a low-slung rainbow camper van; among
ear studs and jerkin, print skirt, gypsy hoops,
a collie on a tartan rug, many children.
We've always stopped here on the plain,
cramped, longing, heading west for home.

And it was worth it after all

After the driving through twelve hours of rain,
the hired Transit van, traffic a nightmare
with bottleneck standstill, worse further on –
police and fire, detours through tiny lanes;
arriving, parking, reaching the pub too late
for lunch, and traipsing familiar, drenched streets
to chip shop, burger joint, Asian fusion, all closed;
returning to the old house, the things left over
and over from other lives, stacked in the attic,
the cellar, back room, his studio, her bedroom;
to dismantle, negotiate the stairs, crook of
the landing in dim lighting, then carry the share
out to the van – the chest, brass bed, blue armchair,
teapot, chipped candlestick, Persian carpet on top –
tying it down and driving back in the dark and rain,
to take it all out again, move it in here, the gubbins
that one day, not long, we will then hand on.

The Share

Old clothes trunk on the attic stairs,
Granny's from Portugal, Teddy's from Brazil,
carved from the teak of an Armada ship,
we were always led to believe. Captain Flint's
with the treasure map inside, or the one
the Swallows found buried on Cormorant Isle.
I want it as I wanted her canary,
her Lady of Fátima figurine, arm around me.
You can't have the Portuguese trunk.

You can. Have it. Remember
how it was the apple barrel
where Jim overheard the pirates
plot, and remember the tower
where David was chased by his uncle,
one stair was missing in the pitch black …
his foot meeting nothing.

Such was my fear in the attic
that night, the story stopped there,
never opened again.
The trunk on the stairs filled
with blankets and camphor.
And there it remains
until some autumn night
we will empty it and climb in.

Subject of Painting

The old deal kitchen table,
stained, bleached, stubborn-ringed.
Posy from the garden in a white jug
for you, the visitor home.

Elaine picked those this morning.
The sweet peas that scent the room
were once for his wife's sketches
and gouaches, her stops and starts.
Teatime talk was the joy of Bonnard,
Winifred Nicholson's still lives.
Then it was what had been left undone.

Her top was the exact colour of that mauve one.
Elaine has gone back to London
and he's on his own again.
Close your eyes and inhale.

A Boat called Groucho

In a photo of the Kennet,
monochrome, wintry, a woman in white
headscarf, short coat, hurries past a narrowboat
where seven cats wait on deck and shore
for the poet's return.

Upstream an artist paints the scene
of bridge and canal on a large board.
Out in all weather, he stabs, drags,
strokes, caresses with brush, knife and hands.
He knows no one in the town
but the poet on the boat
who takes him in each evening.

The painting sings and cries to me
on the museum stair – this meeting of timber,
dark green water, swirling grey, umber and ochre;
vegetation fired with crimson; the slab of bridge
that cuts across as if to hold the banks apart.

I make my way one Sunday morning
forty years later, descend dank mossy
steps to that forgotten quarter – find
new vessels moored along the towpath
bright with dandelions, cyclists and babies.

Thanks to Terry Allsop (the photo), Ray Atkins (the painting *Bridge and Baby*) and poet Barbara Norman.

Old Pennies

In the days of pounds, shillings and pence
there were 240 pennies in a pound,
weighing a staggering fifteen pounds.
I checked everyone's loose change,
took to raiding the bank after school
for a pound's worth in a cloth bag,
carried them home, heart thumping.

Each one inspected for rarity and wear:
EF, VF, Fine, Fair, Poor;
Bun head, Veil, 1912H, 1918KN;
1902 'low tide' with the lighthouse,
a scarce 1926 just in Mum's purse.
Never a '33. Only seven were minted,
of which six, placed under foundation stones,
later appeared in private collections.
That last one could turn up anywhere.

The final minting in 1967
marked the end of history in your pocket
and the bottom fell out of the market.

In the Hospice Shop

The stand wobbles and creaks
turning a hundred old postcards
concerning people, places, events,
unwritten, unsent – their owners
never wishing you were here.
Can they, do they, secondhand?

December Postcard

Anxious her nose should go pink
she dabbed at it in the car mirror.
She moued her lipstick lips, and I in fear
saw her reach for the big dark glasses.
'It's raining, Mum.'
'I know. My head.'
That difficult word *migraine*,
the far away place she had to go.

You sent me postcards of vintage cars
with special stamps, so many trains,
ships and planes that some years
I still send you a birthday card back
in my head. And though yours were half crazy
I treasure them the same.
I just want you to know that,
just wish I could believe you are there.

Her Last Hour

You wait upstairs
for euthanasia, crouched
quietly by the radiator
not sleeping – no more sleep.
We ask you, get no reply,
believe you want to go now,
will thank us for this,
as we thank you for your life.

See, you can still arch your bony back
under my hand, give a tiny mew.
But no tickle under the chin serves,
there's no head butt on the chin for us,
no appetite for it any more,
you don't even close your eyes.

The electric blanket is on.
I carry you over, and as we sit
you start to purr and rasp,
lighter, faster with each breath.
I will take you in an hour.

Common Prayer

Crocodile skin, or from a large snake,
polished by hands, carried in pockets.
It has a front buttoned pocket for the coin;
on the flyleaf my mother's maiden name
in blue fountain pen, 1932.

I've kept it since she died.
She kept it after gran died.
who held on to it after granddad died
in the garage in '51.
They'd kept it since she left home
(the war delayed everything)
and went up to college, married, miscarried,
She'd kept it since '32, we know,
when she was nine and left her home in Lisbon
with her mother and father on an ocean liner.

Inside the pocket, my heart leaps, a coin,
sixpence of 1951 – dulled as you'd expect,
but the detail, the king's hair, also worn,
condition not even Fine.
Put there, I guess, years later.

I search for more clues. The ribbon opens
on Communion – was she confirmed?
Rifle through the Rizla-thin pages for notes,
underlinings, a turned-down corner,
Nothing but hymn after hymn after hymn.

Alison's Lilies

He lowers himself on the chair,
props his lightweight walking stick;
the *Grauniad* fresh from the step
was a job and a half to collect.
Pot of tea under the cosy's another
achievement. The milk is out.
His oats have soaked overnight,
the bread bag with today's slices
fetched for him from the freezer;
cheese bag too, grimy at the drawstring.
On the floor, among biscuit tins,
the crunch of sugar, scraped toast.
What else, old friend? Well, pills,
water, glass for dentures, juice
to microwarm. And the lilies
she brought round weeks ago
are still going strong like her.
He chortles over the obits,
reads them first, will read you one
in euphoric delight should you
drop in. His resolution to us all:
to not fall down this year.

In Summer Don't Hoover

(after Quentin Crisp)

Dust grows no thicker after four years.
Plumbing problems disappear,
they seem to cure themselves with time –
the dripping tap has sealed with lime.
And I move through the apartment without fuss,
scarcely raising dust.

The Artist's Last Birthday

Childlike, he couldn't wait
until tomorrow, ripped straight in,
scattering wrapping over the bed,
the man who

with infinite care
would spend a hundred hours
on one small watercolour
like a fine stained-glass window.

We crowded round, he smiled –
the noble nose, amazing hands –
the paintings now in other rooms,
today it's all paper and string.

We Thought the World of Him

'When my elder brother won his scholarship
to Wilson's Grammar in 1930
he required a medical – I've told you this.
They said his tonsils had to come out.
Father disagreed, took him to Doctor Morgan
who wrote to the school his objection.
Reg went, tonsils intact, came top of the class.
Dad had been right.
Reg was bright,
a chess player, cricket captain.
We thought the world of him.'

Reg Grimstone, RAF radio operator, shot down over Belgium by friendly fire, 14 March 1945.

Quietest Road in England

The road is closed for flood repairs
from last winter, and before the next.
We leave the car on this narrow lane,
rod-straight and unkerbed, bordered
by ancient dwarfish osiers, gnarled
grey trunks split wide open and eaten
hollow from the inside; while sap
still rises up the sides, under the skin.

Under a huge sky built with anvil cloud
you and I slowly walk the grid of dykes,
watch grazing Friesians and their bull,
a heron's flight over the meadows,
wonder how worms survive these inundations
and step down, rein in our angry words
that now might never materialise
like a thunderclap moving off Sedgemoor.

The Outfit

Best suit or casual?
I'd say seasonal, comfortable.

Worn-out shoes or nearly new?
Socks? How about underwear?

He doesn't care!
Just put me on the compost.

    Room heavy with flowers
    bed so cold
    wardrobe full of clothes
    our faces newly old.

But dignity ... look his best ... no one will ... the lid.
Well, he's not leaving in his gardening shoes!

Some of him can go at the end.
Under his favourite apple tree.

Do we tell the estate agents?
How about a rocket into space?

Reaching Out

The long cardboard box carried under an arm,
suspect these days – and containing what it did.
Afterwards, we left it by a bin on the beach

and she retrieved it, brought him back to the car.
'Might be a bit of the old man left behind,' she sobbed.
You hugged her, your little sister, here with her children.

Dusk was fine and clear, wind from the north;
it was dark enough, the Channel a mirror.
We'd left the hotel bar as late as we could,

collected the box from the boot, crunched
to the water's edge, the country's edge,
and dug holders into the shingle.

We inserted the snub-nosed rockets
and aimed the last of him at his star,
more or less (he would've laughed).

Taper. Touch paper. Retreat. Whoosh.
Four times they lit the numinous sky.

FRANK GRIMSTONE, STAR89XMQAKHJG-23611176
Right Ascension: 7hr 50m 29.2s
Declination: +0 29' 17.

Love that Man

For his magnifying glass clipped to the cooker
for the soup of curious flavour

For inventing blackberry water-ice for us in ancient times,
for smoke rings, a gold tooth that never rusted

For re-upholstering the sofa from a book –
washed horsehair drying down the path

For sharing the bacon fat, ham fat, dripping,
his perfectly sliced white split tin

For his pancakes, fruit cakes, marmalade,
the braised meat Sunday casserole

For visiting our mother in that place
and bringing her home for Christmas

For sticking around after she'd gone
with grab rails, frame, ramp and the rest

For staying in our house fifty years
and grounding me, his stepson

The Sexiness of Airports

You find your level, park, remember.
Inside the terminal, search Arrivals
while coolers caress you, heat pockets
flush you, new architecture excites you,
flight boards and destinations pulse through you.
Everywhere, every type, shape and dress,
flesh on show, unblemished skin, perfume, bling,
a strange fascination with Valeted Parking.

Her plane has landed: now all is equal.
Glide granite floors to the barrier (panting slightly)
such expectation on the faces, on yours.
And they emerge in a dream from the mirrored tunnel,
rubber doors sliding open before each trolley,
and there she is, the world across her startled face.

And I Like the Way

she'll nudge the teapot into the sun
save the plastic fish that comes with sushi
give a broken flower its own vase

the way she buttons to the throat in cold weather
folds her clothes on the bedroom chair
and will never, ever be rude in company.

While she returns from Yokohama,
I wash up with care, plant mint for her tea
on the sill, in that same oblong of sun.

First Visit to Japan

i.m. Yukio Imazeki

At a crossroads among seaweed fields
your brother in a funeral suit raged
at handwritten flyers for porn videos
pinned to the telegraph poles,
crying *Japan is now America.*

On the ninety-nine-mile Pacific beach
where sanderlings and plovers run
he ran amok pulling up hoardings
that hid his shrine for Takamura's poem,
crying *Japan is American noise.*

At last among foreign daffodils,
we found the stone: the poem for Chieko,
her mad voice calling from the asylum
to her friends the birds and storms
before the Kujūkuri Business Centre was built.
In his Tokyo suburb we watched *Macbeth*
with subtitles. In his Socialist party suit
he took us to the Museum of History.
His last letter was a rant at Mrs Thatcher.
When the phone call to England came

our blue-papered room filled with sand
from the beach where the plovers ran,
seeing a man die out of a sense of failure.
At the airport he'd asked, formal, quiet,
what had been best about our visit to Japan.

Haiku string

Shark-fin soup untouched,
a clatter on the table
from my dropped spoon

    *

Slippers are turned round
while you eat and bathe and sleep,
visit an old friend.

    *

The toilet seat warms,
buttons hum on the console –
wonder what's in store.

    *

IN THE WEATHER UNDER.
MONTHLY SWEETIES. FRENCH DOG SET.
BOOK OFF. HARD OFF. FACE–

    *

Green Car seats reserved
to the North, the narrow road
recalling last spring.

    *

The great tsunami –
desolation in Sendai.
Grass shoots through concrete.

    *

Wooden snakes dangle
in grandma's kitchen garden.
She settles to work

    *

Slivers of fugu
translucent, chewy, slight taste –
still here to write this.

26.4.11 (Waiting for Fukushima)

I saw the shiny video
of the new shell for Chernobyl
bought by the world's governments
to cover the terrible mess.

A dome of steel and concrete
constructed off-site in two halves,
raised by the world's largest crane,
slides from either side
over the old leaking reactor.

Should be safe for a hundred years.
And someone suggests
when the planet's littered
with these clams,
all the hotheads and scum
could be kept inside them.

On a sunny morning in North London
our baby was kicking in her pram
when the radioactive cloud passed over.
I still wonder about that hour,
the drift that reached the sheep in Dumfries.

Charm of Goldfinches

Here they come on a backend afternoon,
trilling through the gardens, our patch of sky,
a large family living round here now,
new townies on the ridge tiles and wires.
Goldie, Redcap, King Harry, Petaldick,
linked with Hera, in Pliny, in Bosch,
in the Fabritius painting we looked for,
in Clare and Hardy, unchained, released.
Still singing they sweep from holly to feeder,
their stand-in for thistle, teasel and burdock,
acrobats painted with seven colour splashes.
We watch in close up from the warm back room,
then they're away at some hawk alarm.

A Kite for Oscar

Above the roundabout's curve
along these sheer prison walls,
I watch the easy flap and glide,
the hover, cheeky dip and rise,
show-off of a rust-red fork
from the new bird in town.

The Naming of Wagtails

A yellow-breasted one that sallies by streams,
dips under the town bridge, is a Grey.
The Yellow wagtail is smaller, brighter,
a dandelion among the grasses,
in damp meadows, around horses.

The common Pied of car park and playground
is a subspecies of Continental White
with a black back, not grey. It's also called Water,
Willy, Penny, and Polly Dishwasher;
there's a famous winter roost in the Palace.

Yellows are complex, with many races.
My Peterson guide has a plate of summer heads:
Spanish-, Blue-, Grey-, Ashy-, Black-,
which breed with our *flavissima*.
It's safer to call them all Yellow in the field.

Wing-mirror Spider

We've a fellow traveller
arrived from nowhere
to set herself up with us,
accompany every journey
in her hurricane-proof bunker.

The sheer idea of this
sticky gossamer twang
stretched from mirror to door,
rebuilt, renewed each night –
then we go out again,

test her web on a drive into town:
stronger than Kevlar and steel,
for body armour, suture, clotting,
more uses for us than we yet know.
We watch it quiver, withstand.

Opportunists

Gulls wheel over a sea of heads.
Rain turns fields to mud beneath
our thousands of pounding feet,
as forecast. Then a miracle, it dries.
The valley clay springs back.

Music plays all day, all night
on madcap feathered headdress trek
from tent, stone circle, deep-drop latrine
to Pyramid, Other and John Peel stage.
The birds look down and wait.

And into magical dusk again,
their shadows rove a lasered sky.
The frantic gulls can't get through
the fire and smoke, we're so tight-packed
there's not an inch of ground.

Till Monday dawns and bleary-eyed
lines of spears and bin bags form;
tractors come down from the farm,
recyclers move forensically through,
followed by the festival gulls.

In-flight Refreshment

Your plastic-coated paper cup
with its tricky plastic lid
comes filled with hot water.
You get a plastic beaker
with a paper sachet of sugar,
two udders of milk, wooden stirrer,
and the tea-bag, wrapped.
Advice is to pinch the opened milk
or it'll spurt over the seat in front;
put used items back into the beaker;
stow that in your cup when empty
for when the bin bag comes round.
The whole lot's going anyway
to be buried in the ground.
The flight carries on regardless.
Your small thirst quenched, you gaze
at the land that receives this packaging,
the ocean that will receive it years later
as myriad plastic microbeads
that will circle and enter you.

Seahorse

One, dripping in my palm –
soft-boned hippocampus,
curled tail, bug-eyed charmer.
We rescued her with cupped hands
far outside the bay in a Zodiac,
saw fighting seabirds drop their prize,
brought her back to graze.

A million dry in boiling sun
for seaside souvenirs.
Millions more crushed to powder
for Traditional Medicine Trades
where they're a catch-all cure.

Are there more?
There are, remote, in hiding.
They dance in the sea grass
at dawn, she lays in his pouch,
this rarest thing of the male
carrying fertile ova to birth,
and probably their downfall.

The Love

She likes her toast hot
to soak up the butter,
peanut butter, Nutella ...
and dies on the scales,
starves herself, stuffs again
in dazzling alternation –
then she's all over me,
larger and louder than ever,
wanting to swim naked from Uvita
tomorrow – a meal for the sharks –
to draw attention to their plight,
their decimation – for soup –
not for her own glory.

Pacuare Reserve

Out here the great crocodile gapes
like a propped-up car hood, cooling.
We were near her last year's nest

where she ate a scientist
from Tel Aviv who hadn't listened,
swam in the lagoon to escape the heat.

Beyond this sand bar on moonless nights
the great leatherbacks haul up,
gouging deep tracks.

We've come to protect their precious eggs
everything else is trying to eat,
combing the beach nightly by torchlight.

Come to regenerate ourselves this spring,
howl with the monkeys, find the hooded capuchin,
the silent three-toed sloth

and morphos of shimmering blue, pelicans
in formation along a treacherous coast,
piratical frigates above.

We begged Carlos to show us venomous snakes,
the pit viper, coral, fer-de-lance. He wouldn't
but there came news that at dawn

a jaguar had swum the wide river.
We followed footprints into the mangrove –
found the tree that walks.

To the Ocean

This spread and spray, vastness of reflected sky,
intensity of blue. We're five miles up from the floor,
on a wide swell of trough and crest that
rushes from the turbulence of our passing.
We've seen the sun rise, will be here for the set,
another black swirling white-horse night.
No birds for days, no vapour trail or ship,
we search the miles for dolphins and whales.

This heat pump of our planet that circulates
warm currents, this engine for half our oxygen.
Whale excreta sinks to the bottom as fertiliser.
Phytoplankton at the surface is the food base for us all.
Zooplankton rise nightly from the depths to feed on it,
then come the small fish, larger fish, cetaceans –
and maddening humans who don't know when to stop.
These layers of thought add salt to the wounds.

When the income from whale-watching is greater
   than hunting them
when heavy metals in tuna and swordfish enough
   to poison us
when microbeads return in the fish on our plate
   to lodge in us
when five kilos of wild fish to grow one of farmed salmon
   no longer adds up for us
when we understand that every creature in the ocean is
   as important as us –

Sargasso

It's time to stop and make a fresh plan,
a round-the-world voyage like old Josh Slocum.
Find a wreck in a field, make her seaworthy, strong,
name her *Nautilus*, set sail from Bristol alone
with a handbook of your life and doubt.
Biscay's a first test, pray the ship is stout.
Coruña and Lisbon, then west to the Azores
or Madeira, Canaries, hug Africa's shore
south to Cape Verde to pick up the Trades,
crossing the Atlantic the old clipper way.
Oh these heady islands, archipelagos,
cast a lure for the leaping dorados,
tune to World Service, dolphins on the prow,
the sun on your back is hot now.
Over the Line into balmy Caribbean,
keeping well clear of the hurricane season,
let down your hair in the spring Carnival,
rum punch and spliff like at Notting Hill.
The Amazon calls from the corner of an eye.
Siren! Another time, you sigh.
A fair wind to Colón, the old Spanish Main,
Nautilus is raised through the Canal in the rain.
Panama City invites a diversion
to climb that fabled peak in Darien,
look down on the snaky swamps of the Gap,
where the Pan Am Highway suddenly stops.

⚓

Then you're away on a broad gentle swell,
the vast Pacific, life in your caravel.
Not calling at Cocos but straight to Galapagos,
home of Darwin's finch, the last giant tortoise,
stories of settlers on these *Islas Encantadas*,
ménage in the thirties with a German duchess

that still enchant you while you fill up on water
to cross three thousand miles of the Empty Quarter.
Steer by southern stars, allow current, drift,
for the fabled coral islands still on the list:
mystery of Tiki, Gauguin's Tahiti, Pitcairn mutiny,
Stevenson's Samoa, kings and queens of Tonga.
You hit a dead calm, the heat is merciless,
dorsals close in, hammerheads of the unconscious.
Such thirst, delirium, grab a turtle, cut its throat,
drink the blood while you bob and float
into the heart of the sea, its darkest rumour,
echoes of ship *Essex*, mayhem in a whaler
(the serpent eats its tail), and praying for rain,
glimpse a white ocean liner – now you're insane.
Prayers are answered by a savage typhoon
that smashes the rigging; all seems doomed,
blown to the Ellice-Gilberts in parody
of Biggles (or Odysseus) lashed to a coconut tree.
There's no straight line here, hardly form,
just follow the curve through calm and storm,
until you have crossed to a friend in *Calédonie*
spend Christmas in a compound in New Guinea.
Entirely leave out beautiful New Zealand,
land of uncles and cousins removed,
and almost Australia, the fatal shore,
home of a girl who never wore shoes,
a land that remains Unknown for you too.
Like Bligh sailing through with exhausted crew
pause at this sun-baked spit in Torres Sound …
come on, come on, we're half way round.

OK, Harry's Bar, Java, Sumatra, Phuket
all passed the bows, none visited yet
but you will … for something like reincarnation
or some other form of salvation.

Now the return: jewelled Indian Ocean,
Andamans (Sherlock Holmes), old pink Ceylon,
gathering speed now – the way back always quicker
from a day at the sea, the zoo, the flickers
Across to Mauritius where tunny fish come from,
the dodo did, the romantic isle of Réunion.
Great white sharks, Doctor Verwoerd, *Zulu*
still showing at a cinema near you.
To Table Mountain around the Cape,
Robben Island which gave us all fresh hope.
Set compass north to lonely British possessions,
one we marooned an emperor on,
and a final dark tale of circumnavigation
off Brazil where Don Crowhurst's circles of deception
ended in jump of despair from his catamaran
Teignmouth Electron – it still lies rotting on Grand Cayman.
You sail in circles too, stuck in the Sargasso,
in weed thick with eels like a late Picasso
then slip inside the fabulous coiled shell,
smooth mother-of-pearl of a great sea snail
to glide the last leg home over mountain and plain,
the deep seabed, far beneath waves and foam.

Two Rivers Press has been publishing in and about Reading
since 1994. Founded by the artist Peter Hay (1951–2003),
the press continues to delight readers, local and further afield,
with its varied list of individually designed,
thought-provoking books.

The poems in this collection are set in Janson – a lively modern revival of a traditional serif typeface with high stroke contrast and a large x-height to aid legibility. For the headings, we've used Parisine, a contemporary sanserif, to provide a counterpoint to the classic feel of Janson, and to distinguish notes and epigraphs from the poems.

John says, 'I chose this painting by my father for the cover because he is involved in some of the poems, while the sandy texture and interweaving abstract forms are suggestive of the sandpaper and seahorses of the title.'